I0437561

Music Education
Through Gullah

MUSIC EDUCATION THROUGH GULLAH

The Legacy of a Forgotten Genre

Marianne Rice

Copyright © 2009 by Marianne Rice.

Library of Congress Control Number:		2009901450
ISBN:	Hardcover	978-1-4415-1175-1
	Softcover	978-1-4415-1174-4

All rights reserved. No part of this book may be reproduced or transmitted
in any form or by any means, electronic or mechanical, including photocopying,
recording, or by any information storage and retrieval system,
without permission in writing from the copyright owner.

This book was printed in the United States of America.

To order additional copies of this book, contact:
Xlibris Corporation
1-888-795-4274
www.Xlibris.com
Orders@Xlibris.com
58631

CONTENTS

I.   INTRODUCTION 9

II.   The Beginning of a Genre 12

III.   The African Slave of South Carolina...............14

IV.   The Gullah Language and Culture....................17

V.   Gullah Music 24

VI.   Plantation Melodies..26

VII.   Blues 30

VIII.   Spirituals 32

IX.   Relationship to Music Education 37

X.   Gullah Lessons 40

XI.   Interview..56

XII.   Summative Analysis..61

Dedication

I would like to dedicate this book to my husband, Lieutenant Commander Kenneth Wayne Rice; my children, James and Anire Rice; and my mother, Marlena Smalls. To my biggest fans, James and Anire, Mommy loves you very much, and I am truly proud to share this moment with you.

Kenny, I love you for encouraging me to pursue my dreams of what truly inspires me to speak, to comfort, and to love—music. You have experienced every part of the process with me. Thank you for seeing in me what I could not see for myself. You are my rock, and I am blessed to have you in my life.

To my mother, thank you for keeping music alive in your heart and soul. Through you, I am able to continue the legacy of sharing music to the world. Since I was a little girl, I can remember you educating and sharing your gift of music with others. Now that I am older, I finally see the music that flows through you now flows through me. I love you.

I

Introduction

The Gullah culture consists of African Americans who live in the Low Country region of South Carolina and Georgia, which includes both the Coastal Plains and the Sea Islands. The name "Gullah" was derived from Angola, a country in southwestern Africa where many of the Gullahs' ancestors originated, and normally refers to the islanders of South Carolina, while the name "Geechee" has been applied to the islanders of Georgia. "In some cases, local usage corresponds to geographical perceptions: Geechee in the Georgia Coastal Empire and in Charleston, SC and Gullah in the rest of the South Carolina Low Country. In other cases such usage may correspond to generational distinctions: older people in the South Carolina Low Country, black and white, grew up using primarily the term Geechee, which has since been replaced by the increasingly widespread term Gullah."[1]

The Gullah culture has provided important contributions in the areas of art, religion, agriculture, and music. For instance, in music, Africans' expression of improvisation has been a continuing cultural influence in American music, which can be heard in various genres spanning many decades of history. Although one can hear the polyrhythmic patterns, syncopation, and harmonic tones of American music, he may have limited historical knowledge of Gullah music and its relation to American music.

In the American educational system, the music curriculum often focuses on the history and influence of European composers such as Bach, Beethoven, Chopin, and Mozart. When African American music is discussed, the curriculum

---

[1]. Kline, Thomas. *The Linguistic Status of Gullah-Geechie: Divergent Phonological Process.* Thesis, Georgia Southern University.

is limited to jazz, blues, and rock and roll; however, recent studies have shown that African American music originated from Gullah music. Furthermore, the American culture has been influenced by the Africanisms as defined by Herskovits from several West African countries: Nigeria, Ghana, Cameroon, Sierra Leone, and Senegal where Gullah music is derived.

Even though numerous studies about Gullah music have been conducted, some music educators are not fully aware of Gullah music while others are slowly implementing Gullah music in their lesson because of the unsure benefit it may have in music education. This book will reveal and provide information about Gullah music and how it can be incorporated in public schools.

While growing up in Beaufort, South Carolina, I was often intrigued about African Americans singing in the church and in music festivals. I remembered hearing my grandmother singing play tunes around the house such as "*Mama's Little Baby Loves Shortin' Bread*" and *"Michael, Row the Boat Ashore."* As a choral student throughout junior and senior high school, I wondered why we did not sing songs of other cultures especially since Beaufort is immersed in the Gullah culture. It was not until my mother, Marlena Smalls, began the Gullah Festival in 1985 and created the musical group the Hallelujah Singers that I understood the connection of Gullah music—birthed out of the marriage of West Africa and Europe. I personally became engrossed in the Gullah culture, particularly its music. I witnessed the ring shouts, all-night prayers, holiday celebrations, and religious services. As a result, I experienced an understanding in knowing my culture and history that was never provided in the school setting.

Historically, teaching music education in America consisted primarily of music from the Renaissance period, then proceeding to the baroque, classical, and romantic periods. Although European influence in American music is vital, there was limited information about African contributions in American music. For instance, students were aware of the origins of opera but not the impact of African Americans in American music. Is opera the only form of American music? Are students taught how American music was developed?

When there was discussion of African American music, it was limited to jazz, blues, and ragtime; and black musicians were given little credit for their contributions.

"The history of the development of a distinctly American musical tradition and aesthetic cannot be recounted completely without ample consideration of the contributions of black musicians."[2]

---

[2]. Karpf, Juanita. "The Early Years of African American Music Periodicals, 1886-1922: History, Ideology, Context," *International Review of the Aesthetics and Sociology of Music,* vol. 28, no. 2, December 1997: 143-168.

As a music education graduate student and native of Beaufort, South Carolina, my purpose for this book is to inform and explain the benefits of incorporating Gullah music in public schools' music education programs. The book will employ Virginia SOL music objectives and unit lessons used for teaching Gullah music.

> *Until the Lions have their own stories, tells of the hunt*
> *Will always glorify the hunter.*
>
> —Igbo proverb

II

The Beginning of a Genre

Brief History of American Slavery

Since the early colonization of the New World, Africans were involved as early settlers along with Europeans. In fact, the African and the European came to the New World at roughly the same time. "The first black people who came to North America were not slaves, however, but explorers. Among the most famous was Estevanico, who opened up what is now New Mexico and Arizona for Spanish settlement and Jean Baptist Point du Sable and founded a trading post on the Southern shore of Lake Michigan, from which the city of Chicago grew."[3]

African slavery began in the New World in the sixteenth century when Spain imported slaves from Africa to replace Native Americans who died from the harsh working conditions on the Caribbean island of Hispaniola. At least twenty Africans, three of them women, were from Guinea; they arrived to the American colonies as indentured servants and settled in Jamestown, Virginia, in 1619.

An indentured servant was a form of debt worker; the laborer (African) was under a binding contract by the employer (European) for a period of time, usually three to seven years. This was in exchange for his daily needs such as food, clothing, and shelter. Once the period of service was paid, the African could enjoy the same liberties as other settlers. The growing economic rise and

---

[3]. Anderson, William L. "The Beginnings of African American Literature." In *African American Literature*, 133-143. Austin: Holt, Rinehart and Winston, 1998.

---

success of planting, harvesting, and trading tobacco, rice, and cotton made it necessary for Europeans to find free labor. Therefore, the indentured servitude system did not survive and gave way to the institution of slavery in the American colonies. Massachusetts was the first colony to recognize slavery; legal sanctions concerning slavery are found in section 91 of the *Bodies of Liberties*, which reads as follows:

> There shall never be any bond slavery, villinage or captivity among us unless it be lawful captives taken in just wars, and such strangers as willingly sell themselves or sold to us. And these shall have all the liberties and Christian usages which the law of God established in Israel concerning such persons do morally require. This exempts none from servitude who shall be judged thereto by authority.[4]

Many ancient societies had slavery. In fact, slavery even existed in Africa, but the Europeans of the sixteenth through seventeenth centuries established a different ideology about slavery. Many Europeans believed their superiority was ordained by God. In addition, trade and the abundance of natural resources in the Americas (tobacco, sugar, rice, indigo, and cotton) prompted their need to enslave the Africans, thus embarking on a caste system that was supported by race, religion, and ethnic origin. "The five major powers of Western Europe-England, Spain, France, Portugal, and the Netherlands successfully reconciled the traffic in human flesh with their stated religious and political ideologies. The rationalizations which they employed-such as the supposed Negro inferiority and the duty to educate and Christianize so called barbarians-were woven into the white mentality during the colonial period."[5]

> *If oonuh ent kno weh oonuh dah gwine, oonuh should kno weh oonuh come f'um.* [If you don't know where you're going, you should know where you come from.]
> —Gullah proverb

4. Christian, Charles M. *Black Saga: The African American Experience: a Chronology.* New York: Basic Civitas Book, 1999.
5. Blaustein, Albert P. and Robert L. Zangrando. *Civil Rights and African American.* Evanston: Northwestern University Press, 1991.

III

The African Slave of South Carolina

Virginia SOL social studies objective 3.2 states, "The student will study the early West African empire of Mali by describing its oral tradition (storytelling), government (kings), and economic development (trade)."[6] The impact of importing West Africans to South Carolina can be a primary source of teaching students the economic trade of rice, cotton, and indigo in the Mali Empire.

From the very beginning, South Carolina was a slave state. "The first European arrivals were explorers and adventures for the most part. Later, however, plantation owners from Barbados and other Caribbean areas disembarked, bringing with them households and slaves to settle in the Ashley River area and other parts of South Carolina in the seventeenth century."[7] Initially, the European population was higher than the African slave population, "however, black slaves outnumbered white residents two to one in 1720, and by 1740, slaves constituted nearly 90% of the population."[8]

Much of the growing slave population came from the west coast of Africa: Guinea-Bissau, Gambia, Senegal, Sierra Leone, Mali, and Liberia. However, slave merchants of South Carolina often preferred Africans from specific regions

6. Virginia Department of Education. http://www.doe.virginia.gov/VDOE/Instruction/sol.html (accessed December 5, 2008).
7. Baired, Keith E, and Mary E. Twining. "Sea Island folklife." *Journal of Black Studies*, vol. 10 no. 4, *Sea Island Culture*, June 1980: 387-416.
8. Metcalf, Fay. "When Rice Was King." *National Park Service*. 2001. http://www.nps.gov/history/Nr/twhp/wwwlps/lessons/3rice/3facts1.htm (accessed November 15, 2008).

such as Ghana, a region that had gained notoriety by exporting its large rice surpluses. "The Slaves from the River Gambia are preferr'd to all the others with us [here in Carolina] save the Gold Coast . . . next to Them the Windward Coast are preferr'd to Angolas" (Henry Laurens).[9]

Rice was one of the main crops grown in South Carolina during slavery. Africans brought with them the skills for cultivating and harvesting rice, creating economic success in South Carolina. "By the mid-eighteenth century, the slaves on rice plantations provided their masters with the highest per capita income in the American colonies. Because rice is grown in a warm—sub tropical climate, Africans were agriculturally skilled with this crop and African methods of planting, hoeing, winnowing, and threshing rice were used as late as 1865."[10]

Rice was not a native crop of South Carolina, but it had been harvested by West Africans for more than three thousand years. Known as "Carolina Gold," it adapted well to South Carolina's hot, humid climate. "Rice cultivation began in South Carolina within two decades after English Settlement in 1670, and slaves must have been the first people to grow it in North America, according to a 2001 book by Judith A. Carney, a geographer at the University of California, Los Angeles. Africans formed one-fourth of the colony's population by 1672, and food supplies were often short, so slaves grew rice as subsistence crop. Europeans later adapted it to a commercial crop for export."[11]

Indigo and cotton also became beneficial crops in South Carolina. The indigo plant is a subtropical plant that grows at least four feet tall, and its leaves have a substance that produces blue dye. Indigo's blue dye was used in many cultures across Asia, Africa, and South America. "West Africans used indigo for many centuries; indigo-dyed cotton cloth excavated from caves in Mali date to the eleventh century and many of the designs are still used by modern West Africans. Most African dyers are women including among the Yoruba, the Malike and Dogan of Mali, and the Soninke of Senegal."[12]

Eliza Lucas of Wappo Creek plantation became one of the first people to successfully plant, harvest, and export indigo. Her father, Lt. Col. George Lucas, who owned Wappo Creek, was asked to return to govern Antigua and left her in charge of the plantation. "Because the Lucas lands were too close to the sea,

9. *SCIway.net.* 2008. http://www.sciway.net/hist/chiora/slavery (accessed October 12, 2008).
10. Vogeler, Ingolf. http://www.uwec.edu/Geography/Ivogeler/w188/south/slavery.htm
11. Tibbetts, John H. "Gullah's Raidant." *Coastal Heritage*, 2004-05: 4.
12. West, Jean M. *Slavery in America.* http://www.slaveryinamerica.org/history (accessed November 16, 2008).

rice cultivation was not an option so she had to quickly find a cash crop. Her father sent a variety of seeds from the West Indies, among them, indigo. After two failures, she finally produced a successful crop in 1742."[13]

Similar to the foundation of rice export in South Carolina, Africans had experience in planting indigo; their skills complemented and supported the indigo economy, certainly helping to make it a profitable business. "By 1775, indigo was responsible for over a third of South Carolina's income. On the eve of the American Revolution, South Carolina's planters were exporting 1.1 million pounds of indigo, with a modern value of 30 million dollars."[14]

The one crop that remains synonymous with South Carolina is cotton, first brought to South Carolina by Europeans in their sailing vessels. "Men who were unable to pay passage to the colonies were allowed to make payment with 200 pounds of cotton, ginger, or tobacco within two years of arrival." [15] *Gossypium barbadense* (Sea Island cotton) was sold on the coastal plains of South Carolina and Georgia; the fibers of Sea Island cotton were two inches long. However, the process of cleaning cotton was tedious, and Africans had to pick the seeds by hand from the cotton before it could be spun into a thread. Two inventors, Joseph Eve and Hodgen Holmes, developed mechanical devices to speed the process of cleaning cotton. Joseph Eve's device used rollers, while Hodgen Holmes used a sawtooth device to clean the seeds from the cotton. It was not until Eli Whitney's invention of the cotton gin that a more efficient process of cleaning cotton was provided. This enabled European slave owners to plant and harvest at least one million pounds annually.

The Northern textile mills imported nearly 100 percent of their cotton from the South. However, by the end of Emancipation, South Carolina's cotton economy began to decline due to South Carolina's financial recession, a lengthy Reconstruction period, and crop devastation. Cotton plantations saw "troubled times since the Emancipation of slavery. After the Civil War, Confederates burned and Northerners seized the remaining cotton bales. By the time the nation entered WWI, the boll weevil had infiltrated the cotton fields in South Carolina, and cotton farming began to suffer."[16]

---

13. Payne, Jennifer. *Rice, Fever, and Indigo in Colonial South Carolina.* May 1998. http://www.geocities.com/Athens/Aegean/7023/indigo.html (accessed November 24, 2008).

14. (West n.d.)

15. Agriculture, South Carolina Department of. *South Carolina Department of Agriculture.* http://www.state.sc.us/scda/relatedaglinks/boards/cotton/cottoninfo.htm (accessed November 22, 2008).

16. (Agriculture n.d.)

IV

The Gullah Language and Culture

Virginia Standard of Learning (SOL) music objective 3.12 states, "The student will demonstrate an understanding of the relationships between music and other disciplines."[17] In order for students to understand the development of Gullah music, music educators can integrate language art activities within their lesson by implementing Gullah folktales, fables, and legends found in *Gullah Folktales from the Georgia Coast* by Charles Colcock Jones Jr.

It is important for music educators to explain to their students that Africans came from many countries of West and Central Africa, representing many different nations and languages, making communicating with each other difficult. They were banned from learning how to read and write English, which forced them to develop a new language—Gullah. Gullah language is referred to as a form of "Creole" language. It is based on English but includes vocabulary and grammatical elements common to several West African languages spoken in isolated communities from Georgetown in eastern South Carolina to northern Florida.

Tables 1.1 and 1.2 explain the usage of the subject, verb, and verbal adjectives in West African tribal languages: Yoruba, Twi, and Kimbundu. In the West African and the Gullah languages, the subject of a passive verb is placed in the objective; and third-person pronouns—they, he, or it—are placed in the subject of the sentence. Additionally, verb phrases have two or more verbs to express one idea, and one can perform the same function as a preposition, adverb, conjunction, or participle in English. There is the extensive use of these verbal adjectives on both sides of the Atlantic.

---

17.   (Education n.d.)

Table 1.1 West African Languages[18]

	Subject[19]	Verb[20]	Verbal Adjectives[21]
Standard English	Someone loves me.	We are going to visit our mother.	They are friends.
West African	Yoruba: I am loved.	Twi: We are going go visit our mother.	Kimbundu: They friends.

Table 1.2 Gullah Languages

	Subject	Verb	Verbal Adjectives
Standard English	He was beaten.	You better go home go (to) see about your children.	He was mean to do that.
Gullah	They(dem)bit him(em).	Yu beta go hom go si baut yo cilan.	"He mean to do that," meaning.

A mixture of African and English languages, Gullah resembles the speech pattern of the Caribbean Islands: Jamaica, Bahamas, Trinidad, Virgin Islands, and Barbados. Africans, coming from various backgrounds, were faced with the necessity of creating a common form of communication. A few examples of Gullah words used in English today that have African origin are *Bene*, "seseme/benne or benny" (Wolof); *bidibidi*, "small bird or chicken/bidy" (Kongo); *Bukra*, "white man" (Ibibio); *Guba*, "goober/peanut" (Angola); *Jiga*, "insect/chigger" (Wolof); *Jogal*, "to rise, to cause to rise as in joggling board or seesaw" (Wolof); *Jug/juk*, "disorderly" (Wolof); *Na, nana*, "grandparent or elderly woman" (Twi).

Africans and their descendants produced a language that was formed with the vernacular rhythmic pattern and stresses influenced by West African languages. As a result, the Gullah language was often misunderstood for many

---

[18]. Moore, Frances. "Research on Lorenzo Turner; Language of the USA." Summer Project, 2001.

[19]. Subject of a passive verb is used as objective and the third-person pronoun.

[20]. Verb phrases. One performs the function as prepositions, adverbs, and conjunctions.

[21]. There is the extensive use of verbal adjectives on both sides of the Atlantic.

years for this misinterpreted language was birthed out of necessity. "African slaves came from more than two dozen ethnic groups and spoke forty different languages; communication, at first, was difficult." Therefore, they created Gullah.[22] The isolation of the Sea and Barrier islands enabled African slaves and their descendents to keep this language alive and flourishing.

The Gullah language that is spoken today is different from what was spoken during slavery, Reconstruction, and even the turn of the twentieth century. Still, this language is fascinating tourists at present. Yet for the European who visited South Carolina Low Country during the eighteenth and nineteenth centuries, Gullah was peculiar; they often found the sound of Gullah very strange. "No other dialect sounded stranger to white ears than did Gullah. Whites who encountered Gullah for the first time were deeply puzzled by its strange tones and cadences and peculiar syntax. Even African Americans in other parts of the South had difficulty comprehending Gullah. Of course the Gullah that Demus Green used in the 1970s in his animal trickster story of the buzzard and the cooter is not the Gullah that Lorenzo Dow Tuner would have heard from the lips of Diana Brown and Turner's other informants in the 1930's."[23]

Madeline Horres Hantske gave readers another insight into the rhythm, syntax, and speech of the Gullah language. In her book *Songs of the Cotton Picker*, she captured the merging of African languages with English, French, and Spanish by phonetically writing poems that were spoken in South Carolina Low Country.

Waitin' Fuh De Chariot

Missy axed me
How come Ah libbin so long
An' ain't Ah plum' nigh tuckered out
Jest a settin' out hyar
Under dis hyar sun?
W'y ain't Ah tryin' to git some wuk
Ain't Ah know better den shuk' sponsibility?
Heh! Heh!
Missy don't know
Dat befo' she bawn

22. Gregory-Smalls, Cyntia. *Elements that Impact the Retention of the Gullah Culture on the Sea Islands*. Dissertation, Walden University, 2004.

23. White, Graham, and Shane White. *The Sounds of Slavery: Discovering African American History Through Songs, Sermons, and Speech*. Boston: Beacon Press, 2005.

Ah had done wuk nuff crap
Of cotton, taters, an' cawn
To do me.
No'm Missy-Ah ain't frettin'
Bout settin' hyar in dis sun-
Ain't frettin' none-
Ahm t'inkin' whuts gwing be
W'en me an' dis ol' body
Pa'ts company.
Ahm jest settin' hyar waitin'
Fuh Liger an' de Chariot
To gimme a lif'-
Mos' ennyday now he'll be by
An' Ah ain't aimin' to miss
A free ride tru de sky[24]

The Gullah language was viewed as just another form of "Black English," and linguists did not value its importance. It was not until 1949 that Lorenzo D. Turner revolutionized the study of Gullah when his book *Africanisms in the Gullah Dialect* revealed the many concepts and components of the Gullah language. "When Turner's *Africanisms in the Gullah Dialect* appeared, we had for the first time an intensive study of Gullah."[25] Turner explained how many African Americans living on St. Helena Island, South Carolina, located in Beaufort County, South Carolina, continued the custom of speaking Gullah. He also clarified that many linguistic opinions of Gullah were inaccurate. As Turner noted, "most scholars up to that point had viewed Gullah as a more or less aberrant offshoot of various early British dialects spoken by white settlers and servants, with little or no input from the African languages spoken by slaves."[26] Scholar Dr. Ian Hancock further connected Gullah to the country of Sierra Leone. An excerpt of *Gullah People and their African Heritage* explained the two viewpoints:

Many words in Turner's vocabulary, especially those in songs and stories and prayers are from Mende and via spoken by people of the

24. Hantkse, Madeline Horres. *Song of the Cotton Picker.* Orangeburg: Sandlapper Publishing Company, 2006.
25. Johnson, Guy B. "The Gullah Dialect Revisited: A Note on Linguistic Acculturation." *Journal of Black Studies*, June 1980: 417-424.
26. Pargman, Sheri. "Gullah Duh and Periphrastic Do in English Dialects: Another Look at the Evidence." *American Speech*, Springs 2004: 3-31.

upper Guinea Coast . . . cultural links between that region and the coastal island also support the argument: the banjo, rice growing techniques, terms related to music properly took origin from an Upper Guinea Coast Language; especially Wolof; jive form jev to talk disparagingly; hip from hipi, to open ones eyes; and jam from jamm for slave; juke may stem from Gullah joog meaning disorderly.[27]

To completely understand the Gullah language, music teachers must also analyze the Gullah culture. As noted before, because of the isolation of the Sea and Barrier islands of South Carolina, the Gullah culture survived and flourished. "As Europeans deserted the coast in favor of milder climates inland, the Gullahs lived in isolation for generations, allowing them to maintain their African culture longer than any slave descendants in America."[28]

Even today, there are islands that are only accessible by boat, while other islands in the 1930s finally built bridges to connect the islands to the mainland.[29] By integrating their traditional customs into the Christianity of their European slave owners, African slaves were able to preserve and continue their tradition. For example, many Africans assimilated the teachings of Christianity but also incorporated their African practice of worship. One custom in particular was the blessing of a church/home. Africans would pray, sing, and dance once a new building was completed. They followed the singing with shouting. This style of worshiping was known as the "ring shout." Historically, many believed Africans used the word "shout" because it was a sin to dance during worship service. However, Dr. Turner discovered the word "shout" actually derived from the Arabic word *saut*, pronounced like "shout." *Saut* was used among the Mohammedans of West Africa, meant to run and walk around the Kaaba.[30]

> In slavery days they developed a ceremony called "ring shout" in which participants danced in a ritual fashion in a circle amidst the rhythmical pounding of sticks and then, at the culminating moment, experienced

27. Pollitzer, William S. *The Gullah People and Their African Heritage.* Athens: University of Georgia Press, 1999.

28. Glanton, Dahleen. *NATIONALGEOGRAPHIC.COM/NEWS.* June 8, 2001. www.nationalgeographic.com/news (accessed October 12, 2008).

29. Twining, Mary. "'I'm Going to Sing and "Shout" While I Have The Chance': Music, Movement, and Dance on the Sea Islands." *Black Music Research Journal*, 1995: 1-15.

30. Parrish, Lida. *Slave Songs of the Georgia Sea Islands.* Athens: University of Georgia Press, 1992.

possession by the Holy Spirit while shouting expressions of praise and thanksgiving. Gullah culture represents what and why the African did what he did on the plantations of South Carolina.[31]

The form of the shout song usually consisted of call and response. The caller would sing the lead, and the response would be sung by other members of the shout group. An example of a call and response song is the traditional shout song "Until I Die" (see figure 1) as noted in Lydia Parrish's book *Slave Songs of the Georgia Sea Islands* (music was transcribed by Robert MacGrimsey).

Until I Die

I'm goin' tuh set in the humble chair
    Goin' tuh rock from side tuh side
    Goin' tuh rock from side tuh side
      Un-til I die.
Chorus: Un-til I die. (leader)
      Un-til I die (baser)
      Un-til I die (leader)
      Un-til I die (basers)
I'm goin' tuh rock from side tuh side 'til I die.[32]

---

[31]. Opala, Joseph. http://www.yale.edu/glc/gullah/05.htm.
[32]. (Parrish 1992)

Figure 1. "Until I Die" Sheet Music Sample

The song begins with a syncopated beat, and each note emphasizes the words. The sixth measure creates a steady rhythm by using quarter notes and eighth notes for the lyrics "rock from side tuh side."

V

Gullah Music

Virginia Standard of Learning (SOL) music objective 6.2 states that "students should be able to listen and discuss various forms of music."[33] The diverse formation of Gullah music and its subgenres can be a great instructional resource for teaching the SOLs. Africans came to the shores of America with an artistic form of music that was part of their lives. They were able to maintain, sustain, and transform their African culture through music by assimilating the European and North American sounds they heard. The plantation society sought to transform the African into a submissive and a suppressive being by "ways of enslavement, isolation and statements of declaring the African to be absent of culture, and animalistic in nature—so far from the truth."[34] But as the two worlds came together and bonded, it was the beginning of a journey with new discoveries and concepts for the New World. This union transcended the inherited purpose of enslaving the African and brought forth a new and profound musical art form—Gullah.

From the Africans coming to the New World as explorers and indentured servants to the millions of Africans held in bondage as slaves working on South Carolina's plantations, Africans have always skillfully infused their culture: music, religion, food, and language. "Missionaries, slaveholders and other observers from the seventeenth through the nineteenth centuries noted that music was central to these traditions and that instrumental music, song, and dance or some form

---

33. (Education n.d.)
34. Singers, The Hallelujah. *Gullah: Songs of Faith, Hope and Freedom.* Cond. Marlena Smalls. Comp. Marlena Smalls. 1998.

of bodily movement accompanied a range of ritualized events such as religious ceremonies, festivals, and holiday celebrations, as well as recreational and social events."[35] In order to cope with the uncertainties of the life as a slave in America, slaves sought refuge in their music. Music provided the beat, melody, and life force for work on the plantations. This music is known as Gullah music.

As mentioned earlier, "Gullah" was derived from Angola, a country in southwestern Africa where many of the Gullahs' ancestors originated. Africans blended the melodies of their European masters with the rhythm of their West African heritage. Until recently, many historians were not aware of Gullah music. Several factors contributed to the negligence of understanding and learning about Gullah music. Primarily, Gullah music was often considered unworthy of study and inferior to others. Additionally, after Emancipation, newly freed slaves continued to remain secretive about their culture and music.

Gullah is one of the purest forms of music that retained West African and Caribbean characteristics. It also highly influenced what is known as American music. Today, Gullah music can be heard by African Americans across the country, but its primary usage can be traced to the Sea Islands of South Carolina and Georgia. Gullah provides one of the clearest examples of African American syncretism and an original interpretation of religion.

---

35. Crawford, Richard, et al. "United States of America: Traditional African American Music." *Oxford Music Online*. www.oxfordmusiconline.com (accessed October 24, 2008).

VI

Plantation Melodies and Work Songs

There was a time in American history when African slaves were forbidden the use of drumming, so they incorporated the use of hand clapping and feet stomping in order to keep musical time. Teachers can use the rhythmic pattern of plantation melodies and work songs to teach the Virginia Standard of Learning (SOL) music objective 5.4, which states, "The student will employ creativity in a variety of musical experiences—create movement to music."[36]

This often intricate hand clapping and feet stomping distinguishes Gullah music from other musical genres. Rhythm moves it all; the African influence in that area is by far one of his greatest retentions on the world. The drums take over one's spiritual being. The drums were medicine, healing, and communication. "There was a time when we could not use drums but the rhythm, did not cease. We picked up the hand clapping, the foot stomping and the dancing about, and moving in the old African manner."[37] Africans used polyrhythmic sounds of clapping, which consisted of three tones: bass, baritone, and tenor. The bass clap sound was created by cupping both hands together. The baritone clap was done by having one palm flat and cupping it (the palm) with the other hand, and the tenor sound was created by clapping with both palms flat.

Plantation melodies are the first-known songs of Gullah. "They were called plantation melodies because the songs originated from West Africa but they

---

36. (Education n.d.)
37. Smalls, Marlena. *Heritage Not Hate: Discovering Gullah and Finding Myself (Audio Book)*. Hilton Head: Ziplow Productions, 1997.

—

varied from plantation to plantation."[38] These earliest forms of Gullah songs originated from Africa and are examples of West African chant songs that still possess West African words: *Rockah mh Moomba Cum bo-ba yonda Lil-aye tambe I rockah mh Moomba* and *Funga ola fay ah, Ah shay ah shay, Funga ola fay ah, Ah shay ah shay.* (We welcome you with open arms and love in our hearts. We welcome you with open arms and love in our hearts.) The West African musical elements in Gullah music laid the foundation for modern African American music. Lydia Parrish's book *Slave Songs of the Georgia Sea Islands* gives us another view of these plantation melodies as noted in figure 2.

Figure 2. "Rock ah mh Moomba" Sheet Music Sample

Music derived from the pulsating rhythm of the drum has always been a transcendental odyssey for the African, evoking the human responses to life, nature, love, happiness, and pain. It reflected every emotion borne out of slavery. For instance, the work songs, or shanties as they were called, expressed the day-to-day life on the plantation. Regardless of the length of time he worked, there was a song for planting and picking cotton, harvesting rice, and weaving basket. The traditional work song was normally sung a cappella and consisted of three to four lines. For some work songs, the caller would sing the first line, and the workers would respond with the same rhythm pattern.

> Something of the African background of these "pure negro songs" may be gathered from a description of the work songs of West Africa, given by N. G. J. Ballanta, who tells us: Music in Africa is not cultivated

---

38.   Smalls, Marlena, interview by Marianne Rice. *Gullah Culture and Music* (September 15, 2008).

for its own sake. It is always used in connection with dances or to accompany workmen. The rhythmic interest of the songs impels them to work and takes away the feeling of drudgery." He goes on to say work songs are "—mainly rhythmic—short phrases mostly of two or three bars; solo and chorus follow each other instantly; the chorus in many instances composed of two or three ejaculatory words, answered by the workmen. Tempo moderate.[39]

> Cottin need a pickn' sah bad
> Cottin need a pickn' sah bad
> Cottin need a pickn' sah bad
> Cottin need a pickn' sah bad
> Gwine pick all ober dis lan'
>
> Peas an' the Rice
> Peas an' the Rice
> Peas an' the rice done done done
> Peas an' the Rice, Peas an' the Rice, done done done
> New rice an' okra, eat some an lef' som
> Peas an' the Rice, Peas an' the Rice, done done done[40]

[39.] (Parrish 1992)

[40.] Figure 3 "Peas an' the Rice" is an example from *Slave Song of the Georgia Sea Islands* by Lydia Parrish. As traditional work songs, slaves would sing these songs while they worked. The rhythm of "Peas an' the Rice" was used for thrashing the rice with fanta baskets made from sweet grass.

Figure 3. "Peas an' Rice" Sheet Music Sample

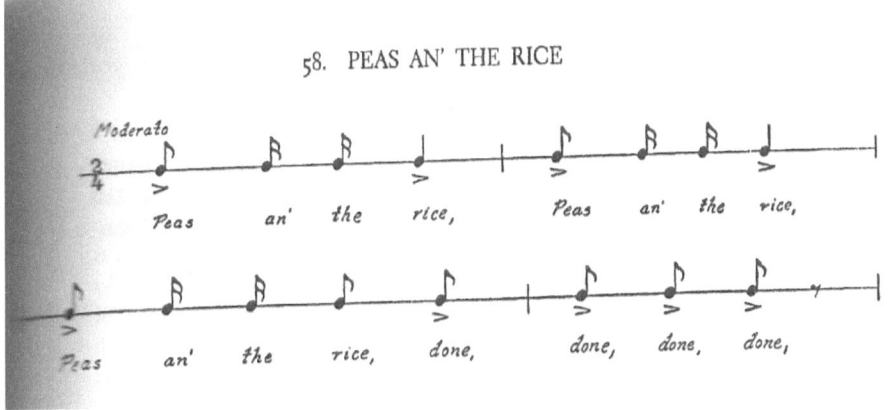

58. PEAS AN' THE RICE

VII

Blues

As written in *A History of Western Music* (7th edition), "the region and origin of blues is obscure, likely stemming from a combination of rural work songs and other African American traditions."[41] No one can clearly state the actual birthplace of the blues, but many have claimed places such as New Orleans, Chicago, and Mississippi. However, the blues also has a deep connection to the Sea Islands and to Africa herself. Michael Theodore Coolen, assistant professor of ethnomusicology at Oregon State University in Corvallis, in his article "The Fodet: A Senegambian Origin for Blues?" examined the possibility of the links between African origins and African American traditions beyond the musical components of call and response, blues scales and intonation, and the AAB form of the text. He found that the largest number of Africans brought to the New World as slaves came from Senegal, with most of them brought to South Carolina.

Further, there were similarities between Senegambian ensembles instruments and the fiddle, banjo, and tambourines in the United States from the late seventeenth century through the nineteenth century. The musical structure of the fodet had a similar structure to the basic twelve-bar blues, thereby influencing the development of the African American blues."[42] Teachers can integrate the history and origin of blues and its relationship with Gullah

[41.] Burkholder, Peter, Donald, J. Grout, and Claude,V Palisca. *A History of Western Music 7th edition*. New York, New York: W.W. Norton and Company, 2006.

[42.] Johnson-Keith, Laura. *Eileen Southern, The Blcak Pespective in Music: Documetation of Black Music Histroy*. Dissertation, Columbia: University of South Carolina, 2008.

by teaching the Virginia Standard of Learning (SOL) music objective MS 6, which states, "The student will investigate music sounds, forms, styles, and genres through listening, discussing, writing, and performing."[43]

Many scholars suggest that blues came before the Negro Spiritual, but there is little evidence to support this theory. They believe that influential to the development of blues was "the collective unaccompanied work-songs of the plantation culture, which followed a responsible 'leader and chorus' form that can be traced not only to pre-Civil War origins but to African sources."[44] The early blues musicians were not typically trained in the traditional Western theory of music but mastered the call and response method; therefore, they were able to create new rhythmic patterns, improvisation and syncopation, and strange bent notes. "Blues often flattened or bent notes sometimes called blue notes, on the third, fifth, and seventh scale degrees, which added to the emotional intensity."[45]

One particular pattern of blues is the twelve-bar line form or AAB form. This form usually consists of three lines with the first and second lines that are the same; the third line is different.

> If your house catch on fire and there ain't no water around
> If your house catch on fire and there ain't no water around
> Throw yourself out that window, and let that house burn down

The blues evoke strong emotions and feelings and is normally defined as sad, mournful, or depressing; but it can also describe the will to survive disappointments such as a lost job, natural disaster, or the end of a bad love affair.

---

43. (Education n.d.)
44. Oliver,Paul. "Blues." *OxfordMusicOline*.2008.http:www.oxfordmusiconline.com/ subscriber/article (accessed November 27, 2008).
45. (Burkholder, Grout and Palisca 2006)

VIII

The Spiritual

Musically, the spiritual is the merging of the melody and form of the European hymns with the rhythm of West Africa—altering and forever changing the original form of the hymn. Virginia Standard of Learning (SOL) music objective 5.6 states, "The student will use music terminology to describe music performances and compositions and identify music symbols within a music composition and explain their function."[46] By teaching musical elements of Negro Spirituals, music educators can model and assess students on the academic vocabulary associated with Negro Spirituals such as syncopation, rhythm, melody, and time signature.

These songs manipulate rhythm and melody. Many spirituals incorporated the hand clapping and foot stomping together by clapping on beats 2 and 4, not 1 and 3. At the end of the songs, slaves would also create a double syncopation rhythm. For some Europeans, understanding spirituals was often complicated because slaves never sang a song the same way. Because Africans sang the rhythm of these songs differently from their European masters, slaves had the need to create and transform songs for each situation in their lives; they were driven by rhythm—the "heart beat" music.

Even though the exact formation of the Negro Spiritual is unknown, it was in the 1800s when African slaves were formally converting to Christianity. Slaves were allowed to witness the worship service of their European masters; however,

---

[46.] (Education n.d.)

they remained separated from the actual service and could not participate during the worship service. Sometimes, African slaves would hold services in praise houses. The praise house was a small-frame one-room building located on the plantation. Service consisted of songs, prayers, and a ring shouts. Sometimes, African slaves had to retreat to the woods to hold their prayer services in secret—the invisible church.

In 1867, William Francis, Charles Pickard Ware, and Lucy McKim Garrison published *The Slave Songs of the United States*. Many of these songs were heard on the plantations of South Carolina: Port Royal, Coffin Point, Fripp Island, and St. Helena Island. William Francis Allen and his wife, Mary Lambert, intimately experienced hearing the songs of the freed slaves in South Carolina.

> The public had well-nigh forgotten these genuine slave songs, and with them the creative power from which they sprung, when a fresh interest was excited through the educational mission to the Port Royal islands, in 1861. The agents of this mission were not long in discovering the rich vein of music that existed in these half-barbarous people, and when visitors from the North were on the islands, there was nothing that seemed better worth their while than to see a "shout" or hear the "people" sing their "sperichils."
>
> The best that we can do, however, with paper and types, or even with voices, will convey but a faint shadow of the original. The voices of the colored people have a peculiar quality that nothing can imitate; and the intonations and delicate variations of even one singer cannot be reproduced on paper. And I despair of conveying any notion of the effect of a number singing together, especially in a complicated shout, like "I can't stay behind, my Lord" (No. 8), or "Turn, sinner, turn O!" (No. 48). There is no singing in *parts*.[47]

From 1863 to 1864, he and his wife ran a school for newly emancipated slaves on the Sea Islands of South Carolina. For this section, all of the songs

---

47. Allen, William Francis. *Slave Songs of The United States*. New York: A. Simpson and Co., 1867.

referenced give examples of syncopation; they are found in *Slave Songs of the United States* by William Francis Allen.

Figure 4. "Roll, Jordan, Roll" Sheet Music Sample

"Roll, Jordan, Roll" has true syncopation that is consistent with many spirituals.

Syncopations occur throughout this composition:

- The first occurs in the second measure on first note eighth.
- The second is in measure 11 on the first note.
- The third is in measure 13, occuring on the first beat of the measure.
- The final is in measure 15 and is similar to measures 11 and 13.

As stated before, the early Christian church in America believed that dancing was a sin. Africans adapted to the "dancing" in the church by incorporating the "ring shout" in their services. Africans believed singing and movement were one and could not be separated. Slaves formed a circle and shuffled around and stomped their feet. Figure 5 is "a very characteristic shouting tune"[48] and gives some insight of a song used in a ring shout.

---

48. (Allen 1867)

Figure 5. "Pray All De Member" Sheet Music Sample

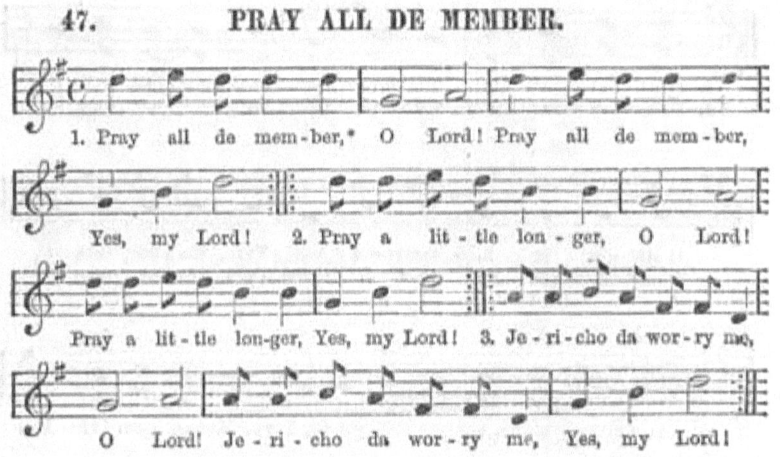

In this song, each word is represented by one note per syllable. Also, in the first measure, beat "two" is accented by using eighth notes. The tempo and rhythm of the spiritual are changed by using half notes for the phrase "O Lord."

A commonly used form for spirituals is call and response. Call and response allowed the Africans to communicate with each other by simply repeating a leader's phrase. During the call and response, the leader would sing the first line, and the members would sing the refrain of the song. Spirituals were also called "coded songs" and usually referenced the Bible, predominantly the Old Testament. The story of Joshua was a metaphor for faith and courage. Other historical figures, such as Moses and Daniel, symbolized the leader leading God's children to the "Promised Land" (the North) while the Hebrew children represented slaves. Egypt was the South, and Pharaoh was the master:

Go Down Moses
Way down in Egypt lan'
Tell o' Pharo'
Let my people go

Joshua fit de battle of Jerico,
Joshua fit de battle of Jerico
An de walls com tumlin down

The spiritual also offered a deeper meaning of death and being free from slavery for the African, as noted in figures 6 and 7, in *Slave Songs of the United States* by

William Francis Allen. "A song "to which the Rebellion had actually given rise. This was composed by nobody knows though it was the most recent doubtless of all these 'spirituals,'—and had been sung in secret to avoid detection. It is certainly plaintive enough. The peck of corn and pint of salt were slavery's rations."—T. W. H. Lt. Col. Trowbridge learned that it was first sung when Beauregard took the slaves of the islands to build the fortifications at Hilton Head and Bay Point."[49]

Figure 6. "Many Thousand Go" Sheet Music Sample

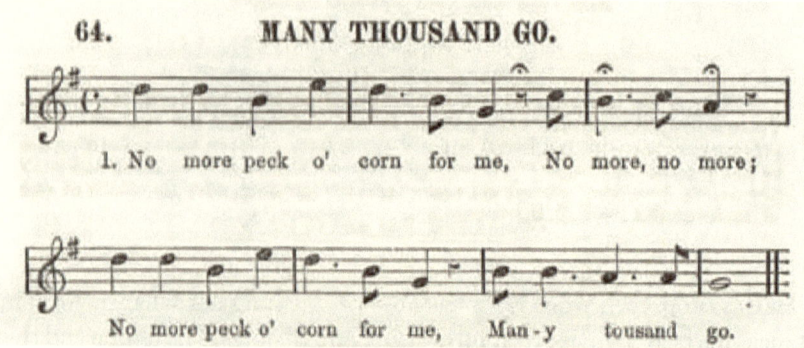

Figure 6 begins strongly with the first word "no" on the first beat. The second, third, fifth, and sixth measures have syncopations and rests, symbolizing unrest and resistance of African slaves.

Figure 7. "Brother Moses Gone" Sheet Music Sample

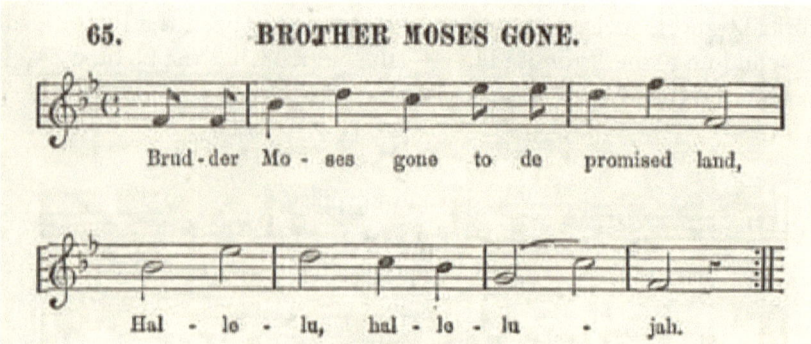

[49.] (Allen 1867)

IX

Brief Overview of Music Education

Despite the growth and the expansion of slavery in the New World, the advancement of music education in Colonial America was virtually stagnant, and the only available music education was through the church—primarily through congregational singing. The introduction to music education developed nearly a century after the first settlement of the thirteen colonies. "There were no music teachers, no singing societies, and very little printed music. Ironically, music in Europe was going through a rapid change-opera, new instruments, new combination, knew forms of writing music and Haydn was grouping the instruments into families and developing the modern orchestra."[50] The New World society was designed to prepare men for technical work and women for domestic work such as housewives or teachers. The early settlers of America were not focused on teaching music in schools; their major and prominent concerns were the daily conditions of the new colony, therefore neglecting the basic need for musical expression.

By the beginning of the eighteenth century, Rev. John Tufts established the first book on singing and used a letter notation *M*, *F*, *S*, *L*, which influenced the establishment of colonial singing schools. "The singing school was an early America's institution and offered a brief course in musical sight reading and choral singing; it was taught by a singing master according to the traditional methods and used tune books that were printed manuals containing instructions,

---

50.   Birge, Edward Bailey. *History of Public School Music—In the United States.* Philadelphia: Oliver Diston Company, 2007.

—

exercises and sacred choral music."[51] The singing school was effective in teaching students the fundaments of music. However, it became apparent that only a select few of students were benefiting from it.

Most of the singing schools were located in New England, but records show that singing schools were developing throughout Colonial America, including the southern colonies. For instance, John Salter was teaching a singing class in Charleston, South Carolina; both Andrew Law, of Connecticut, and Lucius Chain, of Massachusetts, were teaching in Virginia by the 1780s.[52] It was not the intent for the music elite to benefit from music programs in singing schools. Lowell Mason, the first music teacher in the Boston public schools, wanted to "break down" the doctrine of the talented few. "Mason taught music as an experiment in the Hawes Grammar School, without salary, during the 1837-38 school year. Mason's teaching proved, among numerous things, that the musical ear was much more common than had been supposed and that musical susceptibility is in a good degree improvable. That following year, Mason was put under contract to teach in several public schools. Thus, public school music in the United States was born."[53]

Although music education had made great advances since Lowell Mason becoming the first music school teacher, it still did not meet the needs of all students. There were missing elements in music education. For example, "at the turn of the century, music educators were intent on teaching music reading, proper vocal tone production, and an appreciation of European classical music. The materials they used to implement these goals were vocal exercises, composed songs, German folk melodies, and sometimes songs transcribed from the opera or symphonic repertoire."[54] American schools were essentially segregated until *Brown v. Board of Education* (1954) mandated that American public schools must integrate. Prior to and even years following the Supreme Court's ruling, the study of music from other social and cultural backgrounds was not a priority for many music educators. For more than a century, the demographics of the American public schools were usually confined to teachers and students of the same ethnicity and social background, which limited the need for including a variety of music.

---

51. Steel, David Warren. "Shape-Note Singing." *Encyclopedia of Southern Culture.* University of Mississippi, 1989.

52. (Steel 1989)

53. Miller, Samuel D. "Music Instruction In Public Education: Aesthetic and Historical Bases for Evaluation." *Education*, 2001: 41-45.

54. Volk, Terese M. "Folk Music and Increasing Diversity in American Music Education: 1900-1969." *Journal of Research in Music*, 1994: 285-305.

"Because of their largely common heritage, many students and teachers shared not only a tacit understanding of the social, linguistic, and religious traditions of which their music was a part, but only also a belief that much of this music was "great art," exemplifying the highest spiritual and intellectual achievements of humanity. As a result, extended discussion of the social and meanings of the music was thought to be unnecessary or was not considered at all." [55]

During the turn of the twentieth century, music education programs were still missing the defining involvement of Africans in the development of American music. "African American music received slight attention in the schools. Before 1906, African American music was not included in school music textbooks, and those few songs that were published from 1906 to 1916 were often labeled "slave" or "old Southern" songs and represented only a small proportion of the total number of songs in the music texts."[56]

Today, as our public schools become more culturally diverse, it is necessary for music educators to address the needs of all students. Teachers can no longer use Western European music as the only means of defining and analyzing American music. In order for students to benefit from the learning objectives, music educators must include the totality of American music art form.

Ironically, for many years, many African Americans were not knowledgeable about Gullah music. "African Americans can be proud of the many reputable artists and cultural innovators and the African Americans that composed and performed a variety of popular musical styles: ragtime, dance music, salon pieces, plantation songs, spirituals, minstrel tunes, band music, blues, instrumental and choral arrangements, and jazz. For one could listen to traditional African-American choral music in the black churches and the concert halls."[57]

[55]. Scott, James Goble. *Ideologies of Music Education: A Pragmatic, Historical, Analysis of the Concept "music" in Music Education in the United States.* PhD Dissertation, Ann Arbor: University of Michigan, 1999.

[56]. (Volk 1994)

[57]. Taylor, Federick. "Black Music and Musicians in the Nineteenth Century." *Western Journal of Black Studies*, 2005: 615.

X

Gullah Lessons

To further relate the importance of Gullah music and how it can be incorporated in music education programs, I conducted a Gullah lesson at a middle school in Northern Virginia. The participating class consisted of forty students in grades 6-8. All students were given a survey of Gullah music after the lesson to analyze and evaluate their knowledge of Gullah. The purpose of the lesson was to explore polyrhythmic patterns by having students listen to various Gullah songs.

Students reviewed and explained the academic vocabulary words such as "soprano," "alto," "tenor," "baritone," and "bass." They were asked to make up a rhythmic pattern by clapping their hands and stomping their feet. I explained how Africans used various items to make rhythm.

I discussed Gullah music, the importance of rhythm, and explained how the use of drums was banned; therefore, Africans had to find other ways of creating rhythm. They developed various pitches of clapping: the bass clap pitch was made by cupping both palms together, the baritone clap pitch was made by cupping one palm with a flat palm, and the tenor pitch was made by clapping two flat palms together.[58] I modeled the different claps and then had students to demonstrate each pitch. The class was divided into three sections: bass, baritone, and tenor. Each section was instructed to clap on the assigned beat: bass, beats 1 and 4; baritone, beat 2; and tenor, beat 3. The end result was a continuous rhythmic pattern. This is an example of South Carolina clapping; it may vary from region to region:

---

58. Hawes, Bess Lomax, and Bessie Jones. *Step it Down*. Athens: University of Georgia, 1987.

	1	2	3	4
Bass	x			x
Baritone	x			
Tenor			x	

I demonstrated how the standard 1, 2, 3, 4 clap of the South Carolina Sea Islands can be changed into a syncopated pattern: 1, 2 & 3, 4 &. The class continued with the clapping pattern while I clapped on the "&" beat.

	1	2	&	3	4	&
Bass	x				x	
Baritone		x				
Tenor				x		
Researcher			x			x

I played the song "Juba," arranged by Marlena Smalls, and demonstrated the 1, 2, & 3, 4, & clap pattern. The class had to listen and write the various instruments used to make the polyrhythmic pattern. After the completion of the lesson, students completed a survey of Gullah culture and music. Since the lesson, there has been positive feedback from the music teacher and students. The students have been especially impressed with the information about Gullah music.

Gullah Music Survey

1. What is Gullah music?

2. Define polyrhythm?

3. List the European and West African Countries that influenced Gullah music.

4. Explain why Africans had to use the hands to create rhythmic patterns.

5. Identify and explain the form used in Negro Spirituals.

Unit Name: Gullah Journey Grade 6

Standard(s): MS 6.2: The student will listen to and discuss various forms of music; MS 6.3: The student will listen to and discuss music of various cultures; MS 6.4: The student will investigate various types of contemporary music; MS 6.5: The student will explore different historical periods of Western Music
Materials needed for the unit: TV, DVD player, DVD of Alvin Ailey Dance Company, computers (computer lab), samples of Gullah music (Marlena Smalls and the Hallelujah Singers), and PowerPoint slide of Gullah culture and music.

Relative Objectives	Unit Essential Question(s):
English 7.2: Use verbal communication skills such as word choice, pitch, feeling, tone, and voice (SOL 7.2a).	What is musical form? Explain genre. How can culture influence music? What is contemporary music?

Connecting Prior Knowledge: Students have sung and discussed songs of various forms, genres, and cultures.

Summative Assessment(s):	Formative Assessment(s):
• Unit Test • Writing Assignment	• Pre-Assessment • Review activities

Unit Summary: This unit examines Gullah songs and their relationship to form, genre, and culture.

Lesson 1 of 6

Lesson Essential Question:	Academic vocabulary:
What is form?	Theme
	Style
	Form

1. **Lesson Opener:** The teacher will have various Gullah songs playing as students enter the classroom. As they enter the class, the teacher will give each student a name of a West African country or a name of one of the original thirteen colonies. After showing the PowerPoint slide of Gullah art and antebellum architecture, the students will listen to several excerpts of the Gullah play songs "Juba," "Shoo Turkey," and "Hambone"; and the various CDs *Been in the Storm So Long: Spirituals, Folk Tales, and Children's Games from John's Island, South Carolina* and Marlena Smalls and the Hallelujah Singers' *Gullah Carry Me Home, Juba,* and *Gullah: Songs of Hope, Faith, and Freedom.*

2. **Transition:** Show a PowerPoint slide of Gullah art and antebellum architecture. Have students listen to several excerpts of the Gullah play songs "Juba," "Shoo Turkey," and "Hambone." The students will take notes to describe what they hear in the music such as instruments, words, tones, and themes.

3. **Activity:** The students will break into pairs: students with the West African country names will pair up with the students who were given the names from the thirteen colonies. The teacher will provide a copy of the disk with the musical excerpts. Students will listen to the examples again and work together to complete the lesson: (1) make an Excel chart with headings Instruments Played, Theme, Form, Tempo, and Rhythm; (2) identify the elements of the song they picked for their group and write "yes" or "no" for each category; and (3) present their charts to the class for the students to compare and identify components of Gullah play tunes.

4. **Closure:** Review the objective and the academic vocabulary words. The teacher will ask students to define form, theme, and style. The teacher will ask students to explain the similarities of Gullah play songs.

5. **Reflection:**

Lesson 2 of 6	
Lesson Essential Questions: What is genre? How can culture influence music?	**Academic Vocabulary:** Theme Style Form

1. **Lesson Opener:** The teacher will continue to have students present their presentations to the class.

2. **Transition:** The teacher will give each student a chart with the musical headings Instruments Played, Theme, Form, Tempo, and Rhythm. The class will listen to other excerpts of music from other historical periods and cultures. The students will determine if the music samples have similarities of Gullah music and will write "yes" or "no" under each heading of the musical chart.

3. **Activity:** Students will discuss their findings and explain the differences of the various music genres.

4. **Closure:** The teacher will ask students to define culture and how it shapes form in music. The teacher will ask students to describe the type of instrument they hear in Gullah music.

5. **Reflection:** For an extended lesson, students can research Negro Spirituals, blues, and work songs of the Gullah culture and present it in class.

Lesson 3 of 6	
Lesson Essential Questions: What is musical form? Explain genre. How can culture influence music? What is contemporary music?	**Academic Vocabulary:** Melody Form Rhythm Tempo Style

1. **Lesson Opener:** Write the academic vocabulary words on the board. The teacher can play samples of hip-hop, country, classical, romantic, jazz, and blues. As the songs play, have students write their description of each song (make sure that students use the vocabulary words).

2. **Transition:** The teacher will ask students to explain their description of each song. This is to see if students have a clear understanding of the academic vocabulary. Have students brainstorm by making a list of ten styles they like and don't like.

3. **Activity:** The teacher can draw a T-chart on the board and write the styles that students like and dislike. The class will make a comparison of the items. The students will listen to the song "Juba" by the Hallelujah Singers. Once they hear "Juba," students will write one description of the song (students must use the academic vocabulary words).

4. **Closure:** The teacher will review the academic vocabulary words and the elements of style.

5. **Reflection:**

Lesson 4 of 6	
Lesson Essential Questions: **What is musical form?** **Explain genre.** **How can culture influence music?** **What is contemporary music?**	**Academic Vocabulary:** **Melody** **Form** **Rhythm** **Tempo** **Style**

1. **Lesson Opener:** In order for this lesson to be effective, students should choose a "music mascot" at the beginning of the year. The teacher will have a picture of a djabara on the chalkboard. The teacher will remove "Mr. Djabara" from the board, and the class will go on a journey to discover a variety of musical genres.

2. **Transition:** As the students come into the class, explain to the students Mr. Djabara is missing; the teacher will read "clues" to give to the class so they will be able to identify a musical genre and find Mr. Djabara. Each clue will lead to a genre.

3. **Activity: Read the first clue:** Show the picture of Mr. Djabara "singing" on a beach (this can be done with a PowerPoint presentation). He tells the class, "I have traveled to many places so I can hear many types of music. I have to relax, but it is your turn to travel and tell your friends about my trip." **Give clues to the class:** Have a West African chant song playing. "(A) When my brothers and sisters came here, they did not know how to speak English. (B) The songs they sang still had African words. (C) They sang these songs on plantations, and sometimes, the songs were sung differently on other plantations. What songs did I hear?"

   Read the second clue: "I love to hear people sing while they work. It makes the time go by so fast. (1) The form of these songs is call and response. (2) Africans would sing these songs when they had to work in the fields planting crops. What song did I hear?"

   Read the third clue: "I remember my grandmother used to sing this type of song when she had to practice with her choir. (A) The form of these songs can be call and response too. (B) These songs often are called code songs. (C) These songs would give clues. What song did I hear?"

   Read the fourth clue: "Some people don't know if these songs came before Negro Spirituals. (A) People would sing these songs when they were sad. (B) These songs have AAB form. (C) Singers would improvise lyrics when they sing these songs. What song did I hear?"

4. **Closure:** Have students discuss the various songs Mr. Djabara described. The class will do a special project about a plantation melody, work songs, blues, and Negro Spiritual song.

5. **Reflection:**

Lesson 5 of 6	
Lesson Essential Question: **What is polyrhythm?**	**Academic Vocabulary:** Melody Form Rhythm Tempo Style

1. **Lesson Opener:** The teacher can show a brief video of "Revelations" by the Alvin Ailey dancers.

2. **Transition:** Students will write their description of the dance and how the music set the tone of the dance. The teacher can explain that in the West African culture, singing and movement went together. That tradition was carried through slavery. The teacher will teach students the various pitches slaves used for clapping: *bass* clap, both of the hands are cuffed to make a lower pitch; *baritone*, one hand is cuffed while the other palm is flat to make a slightly higher pitch; and *tenor*, both palms are flat to create a higher pitch.

3. **Activity:** The students will listen to "Juba," and the teacher will have them listen to the rhythm of the song. The students will try to identify rhythmic patterns of the song. The teacher will divide the class into three sections: bass, baritone, and tenor. The teacher will instruct each section to clap on a specific beat—bass will clap on beats 1 and 4, baritone will clap on beat 2, and tenor will clap on beat 3.

4. **Closure:** The class will review polyrhythm and the culture of Gullah music. The class will also discuss how that influenced American music today. Divide students into groups of four; the teacher will give each group a song. The group will demonstrate polyrhythm patterns for their song, as well as choreograph a dance for the song.

5. **Reflection:**

Part 1 of Lesson 6 of 6

The student will study the early West African empire of Mali by describing its oral tradition (storytelling), government (kings), and economic development (trade). **Materials:** paper, KWL chart, reading response log, CD player, griot music/storytelling, resource material about ancient Mali.

Lesson Essential Questions:	Academic vocabulary:
What is a griot, and how did he tell stories?	Agriculture
	Trade
What were the major crops of the	Griot
Mali Empire?	
	Oral tradition
How did the export of goods impact the transatlantic slave trade in Colonial America?	Storytelling

1. **Lesson Opener:** The class has been studying the ancient Mali kingdom and Mali agriculture. The teacher will have students complete a KWL chart on griot oral tradition. Ask students to list what they know and want to learn about griots and storytelling.

2. **Transition:** Active reading assignment: The teacher can read a passage about the ancient kingdom of Mali and the art of storytelling (oral tradition). When the teacher has completed the reading, students can write down information that they think is important to know or find interesting (a reading response log is perfect for this activity).

3. **Activity:** The teacher will play a griot singing and a storyteller from the Gullah culture and have students listen. Students can discuss, explain, and describe what they heard. Discuss how many West African stories were told through oral tradition and how ancient societies used griots to tell these stories. Students can write about the griot's tone, quality, and rhythm of the song. The students will complete the "Things I Learned" section of the KWL chart and discuss their findings.

4. **Closure:** Discuss the active reading activity and have students explain the rise of the Mali Empire.

5. **Reflection:**

Part 2 of Lesson 6 of 6

The student will study the early West African empire of Mali by describing its oral tradition (storytelling), government (kings), and economic development (trade). **Materials:** computers, CDs, instrumental music, paper, KWL chart, reading response log, CD player, griot music/storytelling, resource material about ancient Mali.

Lesson Essential Questions:	Academic vocabulary:
What is a griot, and how did he tell stories?	Agriculture
	Trade
What were the major crops of the Mali Empire?	Griot
How did the export of goods impact the transatlantic slave trade in Colonial America?	Oral Tradition
	Storytelling

1. **Lesson Opener:** Computer lab activity: Ask students if their parents have told them stories that were "handed down from generation to generation." The teacher would show a PowerPoint presentation of griot and storytelling, the culture of Mali, and the Gullah culture (storytelling and singing).

2. **Transition:** Divide the students into two groups: For each group, students will pretend they are griots of the ancient Mali Empire (group 1) or storytellers of Gullah society (group 2). Students will write a short story about their family (the story needs to be no more than two paragraphs, and students can be paired into groups of two to check each other's progress). The teacher will monitor and assist students. The teacher will issue each student a copy of an instrumental song. For homework, students must "put" their story to music. The song should be no more than five minutes.

3. **Activity:** Presentation: Becoming a Griot. Students must present their story as a griot would have done in ancient Mali and the storyteller of the Gullah culture.

4. **Lesson Wrap-Up:** Students can write a comparison and contrast of Griots in Mali and the storytellers of Gullah culture.

5. **Reflection:**

KWL Chart

Name: _____ Date:_____

Directions: Before completing the activity, make a list of items in the first two columns. Complete the last column once the activity is done.

Topic: _____		
What I Know	**What I Want to Learn**	**What I Learned**

Reading Response Log

Name: _____ Date: _____
Topic: _____ Class: _____

Things I liked about the story

Things I did not like about the story

What I would like to be in the story

Music Project

Materials needed: large poster board, construction paper, markers, and pencils

Directions: Each group will be assigned a genre of Gullah music (work and play songs, blues, and Negro Spirituals).

Steps 1: Divide the poster board into four sections and label each section.

- Section 1: Genre
- Section 2: Form
- Section 3: History
- Section 4: Group Song

Step 2: Sections 1 through 3 must have a one-paragraph description.

Step 3: In section 4, students will create a version of their group song.

Project Title	
1. Genre	2. Form
3. History	4. Group Song

Name: _____

Project Title: _____

Music Genre

Process	Below Avg.	Satisfactory	Excellent
1. Had clear vision of final product	1, 2, 3	4, 5, 6	7, 8, 9
2. Properly organized to complete project	1, 2, 3	4, 5, 6	7, 8, 9
3. Managed time wisely	1, 2, 3	4, 5, 6	7, 8, 9
4. Acquired needed knowledge base	1, 2, 3	4, 5, 6	7, 8, 9
5. Communicated efforts with teacher	1, 2, 3	4, 5, 6	7, 8, 9
Product (Project)	**Below Avg.**	**Satisfactory**	**Excellent**
1. Format	1, 2, 3	4, 5, 6	7, 8, 9
2. Mechanics of speaking/ writing	1, 2, 3	4, 5, 6	7, 8, 9
3. Organization and structure	1, 2, 3	4, 5, 6	7, 8, 9
4. Creativity	1, 2, 3	4, 5, 6	7, 8, 9
5. Demonstration of knowledge	1, 2, 3	4, 5, 6	7, 8, 9, 10
6. Other:	1, 2, 3	4, 5, 6	7, 8, 9

teach-nology.com. http://www.teach-nology.com/cgi-bin/project_rub.cgi

Total Score: _____

Teacher(s) Comments:

XI

Interview

In order to analyze the educational need for Gullah music and its beneficial relationship to music education, the researcher conducted interviews of individuals who are experts in Gullah music and culture. Each person interviewed was chosen because of her knowledge of a particular aspect of the Gullah culture.

Educating students about Gullah culture has been a mission for Anita Singleton Prather, creator and director of Gullah Kinfolk, a musical performance group. Prather, a teacher for nearly thirty years, developed the educational program Gullah Tru de Arts for Beaufort County schools in South Carolina. This program teaches students about Gullah through the art of storytelling, arts and crafts, food, and music.

Ms. Prather is a storyteller, historian, and actress. In addition to her achievements with Gullah Kinfolk, she has performed at many festivals, such as the Spoleto USA international arts festival in Charleston. Prather's one-woman show *Tales from the Land of Gullah* has been nationally broadcasted. Prather has a bachelor's degree in psychology from Howard University, and a master's degree in education from the University of South Carolina.

The history and impact of Gullah music has been a lifelong journey for Marlena Smalls. Ms. Smalls is the founder and director of the nationally known group the Hallelujah Singers. Since 1990, the Hallelujah Singers have traveled extensively throughout the United States and abroad teaching and entertaining in schools, auditoriums, and festivals as part of their Fa Da Chillun' Outreach Program. Fa Da Chillun' arts program was developed specifically to educate teachers and students about Gullah music. Smalls's music program begins with the African arriving on the shores of the New World and ends with the civil rights movement of the 1960s.

Smalls, a vocalist and historian, began her singing career in Ohio and went to Central State University. She has toured heavily in Europe, performed for the Queen of England, and held concerts in the famed Frankfurt Opera House in Germany. She appeared as Bubba's Mama in the Academy Award-winning movie *Forrest Gump*, starring Tom Hanks. Marlena Smalls and the Hallelujah Singers performed for the United Congress, the twenty-fifth anniversary of the Children's Defense Fund, and for President George Bush at the G8 summit.

Interview Questions

1. What is the importance of including Gullah music in the music curriculum?
2. Are there any Gullah songs that children sing in school but they are not aware that those songs are Gullah?
3. You have been working in many public schools as an artist in residence and teaching Gullah. From your perspective, has there been an increase integrating Gullah music?
4. From your perspective, what are some of the misconceptions of Gullah music and the method of how teachers teach Gullah music?

Anita Prather

Researcher: **What is the importance of including Gullah music into the music curriculum?**

Response: Gullah music shows the cultural diversity of America. Children have been educated from the European worldview of music and what qualifies as quality music. However, the history of our county is not limited to one ethnic group. When teaching Gullah music, students can see the African influence in American music because Gullah is African and European.

Researcher: **Are there any Gullah songs that children sing in school but they are not aware that those songs are Gullah?**

Response: There are many Gullah songs children sing every day, such as "Michael, Row the Boat Ashore," "Shoo Fly," and "Hambone." There are even Gullah versions of European play songs—"Little Sally Walker," "Punchinello," and "London Bridge." Children sing these songs on the playground at school. Therefore, these songs can be easily adapted with the music lessons. However, music teachers need to teach the history of these songs. It is not enough for students to just sing the songs; they must know the history.

Researcher: **You have been working in many public schools as an artist in residence teaching Gullah. From your perspective, has there been an increase in the integration of Gullah music?**

Response: Beaufort County school district has funded a program for teachers to incorporate Gullah music in daily instruction, and some progress has been made. However, the administrative task that teachers must do in order to have more easily accessible resources keeps them from expanding their curriculum. Today, many teachers are concerned about test scores and meeting the demands of daily instructional objectives.

Marlena Smalls

Researcher: **What is the importance of including Gullah music into the music curriculum?**

Response: It is important to teach Gullah music because it shows us that the African did not have his musical and cultural beginnings in America. We can see for the first time that Africans possessed musical elements such as harmony, form, and, of course, polyrhythm. Therefore, it is necessary to educate not only students, but administrators and teachers about this music. For many years, music education has had a limited focus on Gullah music.

Researcher: **Are there any Gullah songs that children sing in school but they are not aware that those songs are Gullah?**

Response: Yes, of course, children learn songs such as "Michael, Row the Boat Ashore" and "Shoo Fly" in elementary school. "Little Sally Walker," "Punchinello," and "London Bridge" are European songs, but here in Beaufort County, many children sing the Gullah version of these songs.

Researcher: **You have been working in many public schools as an artist in residence teaching Gullah music. From your perspective, has there been an increase in integrating Gullah music?**

Response: I have seen changes in the awareness of Gullah music because of the resources and funding for teaching diversity through the arts. However, some music educators still do not have a full understanding of Gullah music. It is easier for teachers to request someone, such as myself, to do a residency program than for them to teach lesson about Gullah music.

Researcher: **From your perspective, what are some of the misconceptions of Gullah music attributed to the method of how schools teach Gullah music?**

Response: When it comes to Gullah music, educators still place it in a box. Meaning, we still have the misconception that the beginning of African American music began with the Negro Spiritual. If we want to see changes in our approach with American music in its totality, we must teach our future music teachers about Gullah music. College music programs are traditionally based on teaching European music, and we need that, but we also need to know about Gullah music. We have few colleges and universities that offer jazz as a major, which again is a perpetual cycle of limited information of American music as a whole. Gullah music teaches everyone that African American music did not begin with Negro Spiritual, but it began in Africa.

XII

Summative Analysis

The goal of this research project was to show how Gullah music could be incorporated in public schools and why it is needed in music programs. The overall analysis of this research concluded that many educators are still not aware of Gullah music, which creates an incomplete view of what "makes up" American music. Historically, the study and teaching of music in schools, elementary through postsecondary, began with the contributions of Europe with limited information about Africa. In order to completely and holistically educate students about American music, educators must review the influences of Gullah.

The African came to the New World and was denied basic liberties. Yet he was able to maintain and even adapt to new cultures. He merged the beautiful melodies of Europe with the rhythmic pulses of West Africa and created a new form of music—Gullah. Today, the syncopation and polyrhythm of Gullah music can be heard throughout the various genres of American music.

BIBLIOGRAPHY

Agriculture, South Carolina Department of. *South Carolina Department of Agriculture*. http://www.state.sc.us/scda/relatedaglinks/boards/cotton/cottoninfo.htm (accessed November 22, 2008).

Allen, William Francis. *Slave Songs of The United States*. New York: A. Simpson and Co., 1867.

Anderson, William L. "The Beginnings of African American Literature." *African American Literature*, 133-143. Austin: Holt, Rinehart and Winston, 1998.

Baired, Keith E. and Mary E. Twining. "Sea Island folklife." *Journal of Black Studies, vol. 10 no. 4, Sea Island Culture*, June 1980: 387-416.

Birge, Edward Bailey. *History of Public School Music In the United States*. Philadelphia: Oliver Diston Company, 2007.

Blaustein, Albert P. and Robert L. Zangrando. *Civil Rights and African American*. Evanston: Northwestern University Press, 1991.

Burkholder, Peter, Donald J. Grout, and Claude V. Palisca. *A History of Western Music*. 7th ed. New York, New York: W.W. Norton and Company, 2006.

Christian, Charles M. *Black Saga: The African American Experience: a Chronology*. New York: Basic Civitas Book, 1999.

Crawford, Richard, et al. "United States of America: Traditional African American Music." *Oxford Music Online*. http://www.oxfordmusiconline.com (accessed October 24, 2008).

Glanton, Dahleen. *NATIONALGEOGRAPHIC.COM/NEWS*. June 8, 2001. www.nationalgeographic.com/news (accessed October 12, 2008).

Gregory-Smalls, Cyntia. *Elements that Impact the Retention of the Gullah Culture on the Sea Islands*. Dissertation, Walden University, 2004.

Hantkse, Madeline Horres. *Song of the Cotton Picker*. Orangeburg: Sandlapper Publishing Company, 2006.

Johnson, Guy B. "The Gullah Dialect Revisited: A Note on Linguistic Acculturation." *Journal of Black Studies*, June 1980: 417-424.

Johnson-Keith, Laura. *Eileen Southern, The Black Pespective in Music: Documetation of Black Music History*. Dissertation, Columbia: University of South Carolina, 2008.

Karpf, Juanita. "The Early Years of African American Music Periodicals, 1886-1922: History, Ideology, Context." *International Review of the Aesthetics and Sociology of Music, vol. 28, no. 2*, December 1997: 143-168.

Metcalf, Fay. "When Rice Was King." *National Park Service*. 2001. http://www.nps.gov/history/Nr/twhp/wwwlps/lessons/3rice/3facts1.htm (accessed November 15, 2008).

Miller, Samuel D. "Music Instruction In Public Education: Aesthetic and Historical Bases for Evaluation." *Education*, 2001: 41-45.

Moore, Frances. *The Origin of Gullah*. December 3, 2001.

Oliver, Paul. "Blues." *Oxford Music Online*. 2008. http:www.oxfordmusiconline.com/subscriber/article (accessed Novemeber 27, 2008).

Opala, Joseph. *The Gullah: Rice, Slavery, and the Sierra Leone-American Connection*. http://www.yale.edu/glc/gullah/05.htm (accessed Novermber 12, 2008).

Pargman, Sheri. "Gullah Duh and Periphrastic Do in English Dialects: Another Look at the Evidence." *American Speech*, Springs 2004: 3-31.

Parrish, Lida. *Slave Songs of the Georgia Sea Islands*. Athens: University of Georgia Press, 1992.

Payne, Jennifer. *Rice, Feve, and Indigo in Colonial South Carolina*. May 1998. http://www.geocities.com/Athens/Aegean/7023/indigo.html (accessed November 24, 2008).

Pollitzer, William S. *The Gullah People and Their African Heritage*. Athens: University of Georgia Press, 1999.

Rhame, John M. "'Flaming Youth': A Story in Gullah Dialect." *American Speech*, October 1933: 39-43.

"Savor the Flavors of South Carolina." *South Carolina Department of Parks and Tourism*. 2008. http://www.dining.discoversouthcarolina.com (accessed November 3, 2008).

SCIway.net. 2008. http://www.sciway.net/hist/chiora/slavery (accessed October 12, 2008).

Scott, James Goble. *Ideologies of Music Education: A Pragmatic, Historical Analysis of the Concept "music" in Music Education in the United States*. PhD Dissertation, Ann Arbor: University of Michigan, 1999.

Singers, The Hallelujah. *Gullah: Songs of Faith, Hope, and Freedom*. Cond. Marlena Smalls. Comp. Marlena Smalls. 1998.

Smalls, Marlena, interview by Marianne Rice. *Gullah Culture and Music* (September 15, 2008).

————. *Heritage Not Hate: Discovering Gullah and Finding Myself* (audio book). Hilton Head: Ziplow Productions, 1997.

Steel, David Warren. "Shape-Note Singing." *Encyclopedia of Southern Culture.* University of Mississippi, 1989.

Taylor, Federick. "Black Music and Musicians in the Nineteenth Century." *Western Journal of Black Studies*, 2005: 615.

Tibbetts, John H. "Gullah's Raidant." *Coastal Heritage*, 2004-05: 4.

Twining, Mary. "'I'm Going to Sing and "Shout" While I Have The Chance': Music, Movement, and Dance on the Sea Islands." *Black Music Research Journal*, 1995: 1-15.

Vogeler, Ingolf. *US Slavery*. February 25, 1997. http://www.uwec.edu/Geography/Ivogeler/w188/south/slavery.htm (accessed November 13, 2008).

Volk, Terese M. "Folk Music and Increasing Diversity in American Music Education: 1900-1969." *Journal of Research in Music*, 1994: 285-305.

West, Jean M. *Slavery in America.* http://www.slaveryinamerica.org/history (accessed November 16, 2008).

White, Graham, and Shane White. *The Sounds of Slavery: Discovering African American History Through Songs, Sermons, and Speech.* Boston: Beacon Press, 2005.

INDEX

A

AAB form   30, 31, 47
adverbs, *see under* Gullah language
Africa   9, 12, 13, 14, 15, 16, 17, 25, 27, 28, 30, 32, 60, 61
African Americans   9, 10, 19, 20, 25, 26, 30, 31, 33, 39, 60
  agriculture methods of   15
  church singing of   10, 37
  music of   10, 16, 26, 30, 31, 40, 46, 55
African slaves   12, 19
  and Christianity   21, 32
  cultivation of   13, 14, 15, 16, 20, 25, 27, 28, 30, 39, 65
  English literacy ban of   17
  resistance of   1; *see also* Negro Spirituals
  worship of   21, 33
Africanisms   10, 20
American Revolution   16
Americans
  cultural diversity of   59
  education of   9, 11, 38, 39, 59, 60, 61
  music of   9, 10, 16, 25, 27, 30, 39, 43, 49, 51, 59, 60, 61, 63
Angola   9, 15, 18, 25

B

baritone clap; *see also* Gullah music
bass clap; *see also* Gullah music
Beaufort County   10, 11, 20, 56, 60
bent notes   31; *see also* blues
blues   10, 16, 26, 30, 31, 40, 46, 55; *see also* bent notes
Brown v. Board of Education   38

C

call and response   22, 30, 31, 35, 47
Chain, Lucius   38
choral singing
chorus; *see also* Gullah music
Christian evangelization   13
Coastal Plains   9, 16
Colonial America   12, 13, 15, 24, 30, 37, 38, 50, 51, 59
  Bodies of Liberties   13
  Christian churches   34
  music elite   38
  slavery   12, 13, 16, 21
congregational singing
conjunctions, *see under* Gullah language
Coolen, Michael Theodore
  "Fodet, The"   30

cotton farming   13, 14, 15, 16, 19, 20,
  27, 64
Creole language, *see* Gullah language

D

Daniel (biblical)   35
death   36
divine law   13
djabara   47, 48, 49
double syncopation rhythm   32

F

Fa Da Chillun' Outreach Program   56, 57
"Fodet, The" (Coolen)   30
foot stomping   32
Francis, William
  The Slave Songs of the United States   33

G

Garrison, Lucy McKim
  The Slave Songs of the United States   33
Geechee   9; *see also* Gullah
Georgia   9, 16, 17, 22, 24, 25, 27, 28, 39,
  40, 41, 63
Georgia Coastal Empire   9
griot music   50, 51
Gullah culture   9, 10, 19, 21, 22, 27, 41,
  43, 45, 46, 50, 51, 56, 63
Gullah Festival   10
Gullah Folktales from the Georgia Coast
  (Jones)   17
Gullah Kinfolk   56
Gullah language   17, 18, 19, 20, 21
  adverbs   17, 18
  Africanisms   20
  animal trickster story   19
  cadences   19
  conjunctions   18

folktales   17
passive verb subject   18
verb phrases   17, 18
verbs   17
Gullah Music   9, 10, 17, 24, 25, 26, 27,
  39, 40, 42, 43, 45, 56, 59, 60, 61
baritone clap   40
bass clap   26, 40
call and response song   22
a cappella   27
and European play songs   59
instruments in   30, 37, 41, 44, 45
interpretation of religion   26
musicians of, *see specific names of
  individual musicians*
polyrhythmic patterns   41
syncopation   14, 32, 34
syncretism   26
tenor clap   26, 40, 41, 49, 60
work songs   26, 27, 28, 30, 46
Gullah People and Their African Heritage
  (Hancock)   20, 24, 63
Gullah Tru de Arts   56

H

"Hambone"
Hancock, Ian   20
  Gullah People and their African Heritage   20
hand clapping
Hantske, Madeline Horres
  Songs of the Cotton Picker   19
Hawes Grammar School   38
Hebrew children   35

I

indentured servants   12, 24; *see also*
  African slaves
interviews   27, 56, 58, 65
Israel (biblical)   13

J

jazz 10, 39, 40, 46, 60, 61
Jones, Charles Colcock, Jr.
  Gullah Folktales from the Georgia Coast 17
Joshua (biblical) 35
"Juba" 41, 44, 46, 49

L

"Little Sally Walker" 59, 60
"London Bridge" 59, 60

M

Mali Empire 14, 50, 51
  economic development of 43, 50
  government of 14, 50, 51
  oral tradition of 14, 50, 51
"Mama's Little Baby Loves Shortin'
    Bread" 10
Marlena Smalls and the Hallelujah
    Singers 10, 32, 43, 44, 47, 57, 58
Mason, Lowell 38
"Michael, Row the Boat Ashore" 10, 59, 60
Mohammedans 21
Moses (biblical) 20, 35
musical sight reading 37

N

Negro Spirituals 32, 35, 36, 49, 55, 61;
  see also blues; Gullah music

O

opera 10, 37, 38, 57

P

Parrish, Lydia
  Slave Songs of the Georgia Sea Islands
    21, 22, 23, 27, 28, 64

participles, *see under* Gullah language
plantation melodies 26, 27; *see also*
    Gullah music
plantation society 24
praise houses 33
Prather, Anita Singleton 56, 59
prepositions, *see under* Gullah language
public school music 38, 63; *see also*
    American education
"Punchinello" 59, 60

R

ragtime 10, 39
ring shout 33, 34, 35; *see also* Gullah
    music
rock and roll 10

S

salon pieces 39
Salter, John 38
saut 21
Sea Islands 9, 10, 16, 19, 21, 22, 25, 27,
    28, 30, 33, 34, 63, 65
"Shoo Fly" 59, 60
"Shoo Turkey" 44
shout song 10, 21, 22, 33, 34; *see also*
    Gullah music
sin of dancing 21
Slave Songs of the Georgia Sea Islands
    (Parrish) 22
Slave Songs of the United States, The
    (Francis et al.) 33
Smalls, Marlena 7, 10, 21, 24, 25, 41,
    43, 44, 56, 57, 58, 60, 64
SOL (Standard of Learning) 11, 13,
    14, 16, 17, 24, 26, 28, 31, 32, 43
Songs of the Cotton Picker (Hantske) 19
South Carolina 9, 10, 11, 14, 15, 16, 19,
    20, 22, 26, 30, 33, 38, 44, 56, 64
spiritual possession 22

T

tenor clap   26, 40, 41, 49, 60; *see also*
   Gullah music

V

verbs, *see under* Gullah language
villinage   13
Virginia Standard of Learning, *see*
   Standard of Learning

W

"Waitin' Fuh De Chariot"   19
Wappo Creek plantation   15
Ware, Charles Pickard
   The Slave Songs of the United States   33
work songs   26, 27, 28, 30, 45, 48; *see
   also* Gullah music

www.ingramcontent.com/pod-product-compliance
Lightning Source LLC
Chambersburg PA
CBHW031326290526
45784CB00014B/2280